When I Was Young

SCHOOL LIFE
IN THE 1940s and 50s

Faye Gardner with Anne Richardson

Evans

First published in this edition in 2012 by Evans Brothers Ltd
2A Portman Mansions
Chiltern St
London W1U 6NR

www.evansbooks.co.uk

British Library Cataloguing in Publication Data

Gardner, Faye.
School life in the 1940s and 50s. — (When I was young)
1. School children—Great Britain—Juvenile literature.
2. Schools—Great Britain—History—20th century—
Juvenile literature. 3. Great Britain—Social life and
customs—20th century—Juvenile literature.
I. Title II. Series III. Richardson, Anne, 1942-
371'.00941'09044-dc22

ISBN-13: 9780237543860

Acknowledgements
Planning and production by Discovery Books Limited
Edited by Faye Gardner
Commissioned photography by Gerry McKann and Morris Nessam
Designed by Calcium

The publisher would like to thank Anne Richardson for her kind help in the preparation of this book.

For permission to reproduce copyright material, the author and publishers gratefully acknowledge the following: Beamish, The North of England Open Air Museum, County Durham: 9 (bottom right), 10, 11 (top), 12 (centre), 14, 17 (bottom), 18, 22 (top); Durham Record Office: 7 (centre); Hulton Getty: cover, 16 (bottom), 19 (top), 20 (bottom), 21, 26; Olive Linge: 7 (top); Topham Picturepoint: 9 (centre left), 22 (bottom), 23.

Contents

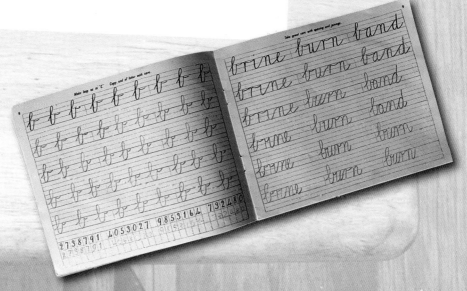

'I was born in 1942.'

My name is Anne, and I enjoy talking to my family about when I was young. Today I'm telling Robbie, who is two and a half years old, about school life in the 1940s and 50s.

I was born in 1942 during the Second World War. When I was young I lived in a village called Willington, which is in the north of England.

The village was built around a big coal pit. You can see the pile of coal **slag** in this picture. My father was a coal miner and my mother was a housewife. All my friends' dads were miners, too.

I started school when I was five years old, two years after the war had ended. I am going to tell you about my school and how things were different for school children in those days.

'The schools were built in 1879'

My first school was called Willington Infants. When I was seven I moved to the junior school, which was next door to the infants. The schools were built in 1879, out of red brick made in the village. They had the date they were built written on them.

Each school had its own headmaster. You can see my junior school headmaster in this picture. I am sitting near him in the

second row. He lived in a house next to the school. There was a beautiful garden where we sometimes had gardening lessons.

Boys and girls had separate entrances to each school. Each entrance had GIRLS or BOYS carved above the door in stone. Every morning a teacher stood at each entrance to make sure that we used the right one.

'We weren't allowed to move.'

There were nearly fifty children in my class! We sat in pairs behind wooden desks. The desks had lids and space inside for us to keep our books and pens. The teacher had her own desk at the front of the class.

During lessons we weren't allowed to move from our seats. When we finished our work, we put up a hand and waited for the teacher to come to our desk.

The walls of my classroom were bare apart from one or two charts like these, and a large blackboard. The room was heated by an open fire at the front of the class. If you were in the back row it didn't keep you very warm! The fire was looked after by the **caretaker**. Every couple of hours he came to put on more coal, which he carried in a large metal bucket.

My school had a big hall where we had PE lessons and put on a play each year.

Here I am with my class, in a play called *The Fairies of Bluebell Wood*.

'Teachers were very strict.'

Teachers were very strict and most classwork had to be done in silence. Anyone caught talking was punished straight away. In those days teachers used to smack children across the hands with a cane or a leather strap like these. It was very painful! Teachers often punished children for being lazy or for making mistakes in their work, too.

This is a photo of one of my teachers. Her name was Miss Tunstall. All of my teachers were women. During the war many male teachers had left their jobs to join the **armed forces**. None of my teachers was married because women teachers weren't allowed to get married in those days.

My favourite teacher was called Miss Walls. She had lots of pet animals and sometimes brought them to school to show her pupils. In this photo you can see her with her pet dog.

This photo was taken in May 1950. Willington football team had just won a cup and the goalkeeper brought it to my school to have a picture taken. You can see the cup in the front of the photo and the goalkeeper at the back. I'm sitting near the cup in the second row.

'We wrote with steel-nibbed pens.'

School started with a half-hour **assembly** in the hall. We had to sit cross-legged on the floor while the headmaster read out a story from the Bible. Afterwards we stood to say prayers, a teacher played the piano and we sang hymns.

Every morning we had lessons in sums, reading and handwriting. We wrote with steel-nibbed pens which had to be dipped in ink. It was much messier than writing with a ball-point pen! The **nibs** were scratchy and made splodges of ink on the paper.

During handwriting lessons we wrote in exercise books like this one. We had to fit letters between the lines on the page neatly. It took a lot of concentration!

I kept my pens in a wooden pencil box made by my granddad. It had a sliding top like this one, but my box also had a little compartment to keep new nibs.

'We had top and whip races.'

At playtime we went outside to play in the playground. There was always a teacher on duty. We played hopscotch with an old tobacco tin filled with pebbles. Some children collected picture cards from cigarette packets and brought them to school to swap with friends.

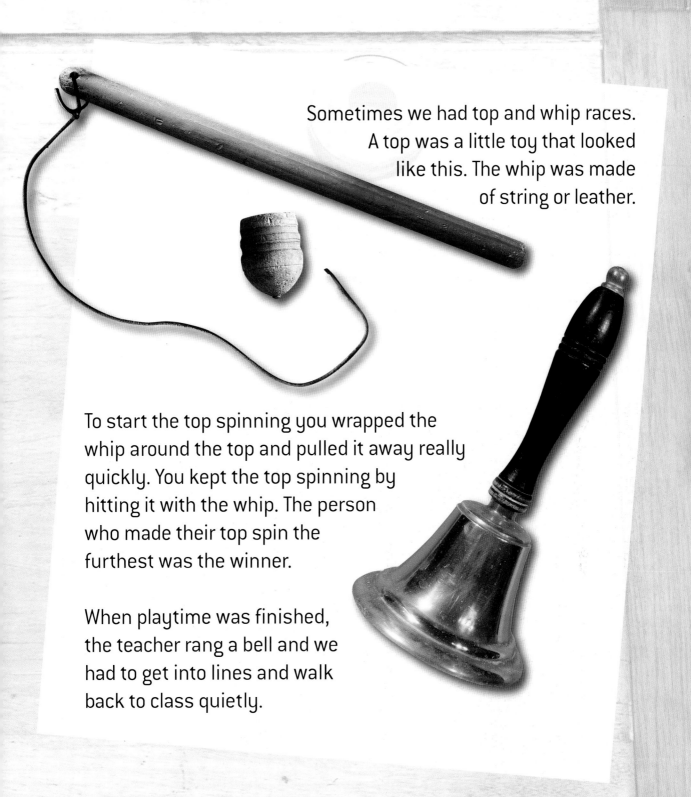

Sometimes we had top and whip races. A top was a little toy that looked like this. The whip was made of string or leather.

To start the top spinning you wrapped the whip around the top and pulled it away really quickly. You kept the top spinning by hitting it with the whip. The person who made their top spin the furthest was the winner.

When playtime was finished, the teacher rang a bell and we had to get into lines and walk back to class quietly.

'We didn't have many books.'

In those days schools didn't have computers or televisions. Some schools had **wireless** sets and children often listened to radio programmes as part of their lessons.

At my school we had a jumble sale to make money to buy a wireless. It took a whole year to collect enough things for the sale, and we made a total of £70. That was a lot of money in those days!

We didn't have many books so we had to copy things off the blackboard and learn them by heart. During reading lessons we had to share one book between the whole class! Each pupil had to read a few lines aloud then pass the book to the next person.

We read adventure stories like *The Arabian Nights*, *Peter Pan*, and *Robin Hood And His Merry Men*.

'Children got a free drink of milk.'

In those days most people were less well off than they are now. At my school we didn't have to wear uniforms because most children couldn't afford them. Here I am wearing a jumper that my mum knitted out of wool unpicked from old jumpers.

The government tried to help children by giving them free school dinners.

For many children school dinners were the only hot meal they would get that day! The dinners were cooked in a big kitchen at the

school. We usually had meat and mashed potato, with jam sponge for pudding.

Children got a free drink of milk at school, too. The milk came in 1/3 pint bottles (less than a quarter litre), with straws stuck in the top. The caretaker brought the bottles to our

classroom in big wooden crates. When we finished our milk we put the empty bottles back in the crates for the caretaker to take away.

'We learned about the British Empire.'

Most afternoons we had lessons in geography or history. In geography we learned about the countries of the **British Empire** and Europe. We used a globe, like this one, to learn the names of the capital cities and main rivers of each country by heart.

I liked history because we learned about **explorers** and their exciting journeys. When I was eleven, we did a project on two explorers called Edmund Hillary and Tenzing Norgay. They had just climbed to the top of Mount Everest, the highest mountain in the world.

Every Friday the teacher gave us a test on everything we had learned that week.

Three times a week we had PE. The lessons were in the hall because we didn't have a playing field. There wasn't much sports equipment. We spent most of the lesson doing exercises and jumping on the spot.

'Every child had to take an exam.'

When I was young every child had to take an exam called the 11 Plus in their last year at junior school. If you passed the 11 Plus exam, you could go to a grammar school. I went to grammar school in a town near my village called Wolsingham.

The photo above shows the old entrance to the school. The writing on the bricks tells you the school first opened in 1614.

24

At grammar school we had to wear navy uniforms and the teachers wore long, black gowns and flat, square hats called mortar boards. The photo below was taken during my last year at grammar school. I'm in the front row, on the left.

Before the war, most children left school at fourteen to get a job. After the war, the government made a new rule which said children had to go to school until they were fifteen years old.

'Children were given school prizes.'

At grammar school we studied subjects we had never learned before like French, cookery and science. My favourite subject was chemistry.

Each subject was taught in a different classroom so we moved about quite a lot. The classrooms had tables instead of desks so we had to carry our books around in satchels.

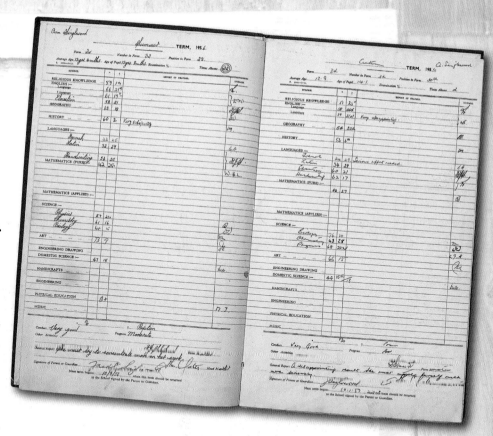

At the end of each term we had exams in every subject. The results were written in report books which we had to take home to our parents.

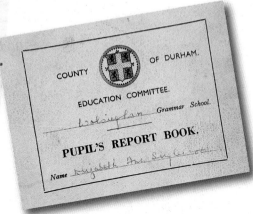

This report says I've had too many days off school and I need to work harder!

Children who got high marks were sometimes given school prizes as a reward. When I was fifteen I won a book for getting top marks in science.

My grammar school had its own magazine called *The Phoenix*, which was written by pupils at the school.

'We had time to enjoy ourselves, too.'

School time wasn't just about doing lessons and exams: we had time to enjoy ourselves, too.

This is a picture of me at my sixth birthday party with some of my friends from school.

Here I am having fun in a school play with some girls from my class.

Glossary

Armed forces The army, navy or airforce.

Assembly When all the pupils and teachers in a school come together, usually to sing songs and say a prayer.

British Empire A group of countries that used to be ruled by Britain, like India and parts of Africa.

Caretaker A person who looks after the school buildings.

Explorer A person who travels to parts of the world to find out more about the land, the people and wildlife that live there.

Nib The metal point of a pen.

Slag The waste from a coal mine.

Wireless A radio.

Useful books and websites

There are lots of books to read and websites to visit to learn more about school life in the 1940s and 50s. Here are a few to get you started:

www.bbc.co.uk/ww2peopleswar/stories/29/a1096229.shtml
Read about one lady's memories of school life during the Second World War.

www.movinghistory.ac.uk/homefront/films/se2.html
www.movinghistory.ac.uk/homefront/films/wx2.html
See clips from footage of children at school during the Second World War.

www.middlestreet.org/mshistory/1940s.htm
Look at pictures of school life in the 1940s.

www.bbc.co.uk/schools/primaryhistory/world_war2/growing_up_in_wartime/
Learn about growing up in wartime.

Britain since 1930 (Britain through the Ages), Stewart Ross, Evans 2003
School Life (In the War), Peter Hicks, Wayland 2008
Evacuation (At Home in World War Two), Stewart Ross, Evans 2007

Activities and cross-curricular work

Activities suggested on this page support progression in learning by consolidating and developing ideas from the book and helping the children to link the new concepts with their own experiences. Making these links is crucial in helping young children to engage with learning and to become lifelong learners.

Ideas on the next page develop essential skills for learning by suggesting ways of making links across the curriculum and in particular to literacy, numeracy and ICT.

Word Panel

Check that the children know the meaning of each of these words and ideas from the book, in addition to the words in the glossary.

- Afterwards
- Ago
- Before
- Bible
- Blackboard
- Coal pit
- Desk
- Grammar school
- Hopscotch
- Hymns
- Infant school
- Ink
- Junior school
- Miner
- Open fire
- Second World War

Research Questions

Once you have read and discussed the book, ask groups of children to talk together and think of more information they would like to know. Can they suggest where to look for the answers?

Comparing Schools

Have any of the children ever been to a different school? Ask them to list some of the things that are different and some that are the same in both schools.

- Try to make links with a school in the UK which is different from yours.
- Help children to compile lists of questions to ask.
- If your school is less than 50 years old, find out about what schools look like that were built more than 50 years ago.
- Talk about how the school building impacts on the curriculum you can offer, the working spaces and the displays on the walls.

- What do children think of the idea of separate entrances for boys and girls? How about separate playgrounds? Are there any schools which still use separate entrances?
- Use the internet to find images of old and modern schools. Make a display showing how they differ and what this means to the children inside.

Teaching and Learning

What can children find out about classroom life in the 1940s and 50s from the book? What other questions would they like to ask?

- Talk about who they can ask or where the information might come from.
- Encourage them to ask their parents, grandparents and great-grandparents about their school lives.
- Do they still have books and resources from that time? If so, how are they different from those we use today?
- Visit libraries and museums to find copies of old books for children. Are they more appealing to read than books today?
- Talk to the children about your own experience of schooling, even though it was unlikely to have been in the 1940s! What has changed since you were at school?

Working Together

Take the opportunity to talk to the children about how we keep a happy classroom. In the book, the children were punished for talking by the strap or cane.

- Talk about how all children might feel in the classroom if they knew that they would be hit for talking.
- How would they feel about other, disruptive, children being hit when they were disruptive?
- Suggest that the children write a 'classroom charter', explaining what they think behaviour should be like and how misdemeanours should be punished. (Clarify that corporal punishment can't be part of it!)

Using 'School Life in the 1940s and 50s' for cross-curricular work

The web below indicates some areas for cross-curricular study. Others may well come from your own class's engagement with the ideas in the book.

The activities suggested will help children to develop key competencies as:

- successful learners
- confident individuals and
- responsible citizens.

Cross-curricular work is particularly beneficial in developing the thinking and learning skills that contribute to building these competencies because it encourages children to make links, to transfer learning skills and to apply knowledge from one context to another. As importantly, cross-curricular work can help children to understand how school work links to their daily lives. For many children, this is a key motivation in becoming a learner.

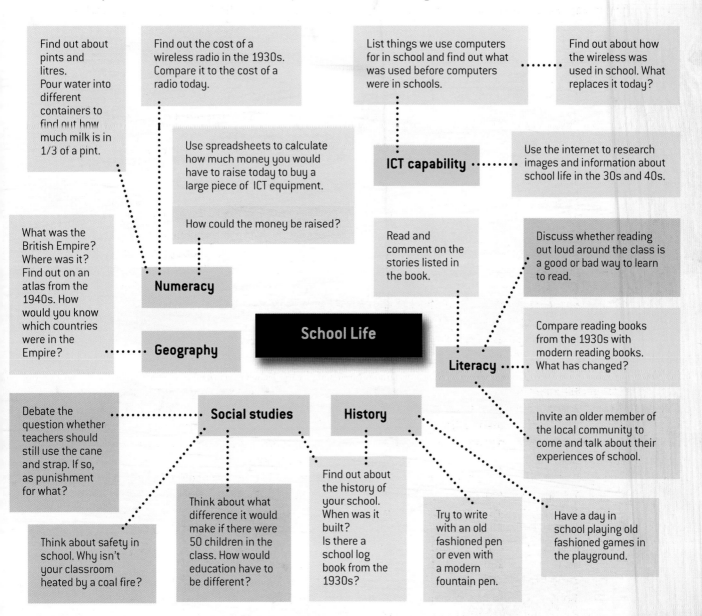

Find out about pints and litres. Pour water into different containers to find out how much milk is in 1/3 of a pint.

Find out the cost of a wireless radio in the 1930s. Compare it to the cost of a radio today.

List things we use computers for in school and find out what was used before computers were in schools.

Find out about how the wireless was used in school. What replaces it today?

Use spreadsheets to calculate how much money you would have to raise today to buy a large piece of ICT equipment.

How could the money be raised?

ICT capability

Use the internet to research images and information about school life in the 30s and 40s.

What was the British Empire? Where was it? Find out on an atlas from the 1940s. How would you know which countries were in the Empire?

Numeracy

Read and comment on the stories listed in the book.

Discuss whether reading out loud around the class is a good or bad way to learn to read.

Geography

School Life

Compare reading books from the 1930s with modern reading books. What has changed?

Literacy

Debate the question whether teachers should still use the cane and strap. If so, as punishment for what?

Social studies

History

Invite an older member of the local community to come and talk about their experiences of school.

Think about safety in school. Why isn't your classroom heated by a coal fire?

Think about what difference it would make if there were 50 children in the class. How would education have to be different?

Find out about the history of your school. When was it built? Is there a school log book from the 1930s?

Try to write with an old fashioned pen or even with a modern fountain pen.

Have a day in school playing old fashioned games in the playground.

Key   Successful learners   Confident individuals   Responsible citizens

Index